The Library of
HOLIDAYS™

Veterans Day

Leslie C. Kaplan

The Rosen Publishing Group's
PowerKids Press™
New York

To the Candy Cane Kid

Published in 2004 by The Rosen Publishing Group, Inc.
29 East 21st Street, New York, NY 10010

First Edition

Editor: Jannell Khu

Book Design: Michael J. Caroleo and Michael de Guzman

Layout Design: Nick Sciacca

Photo Credits: Cover, p. 4 © Joseph Sohm; ChromoSohm Inc./CORBIS; p. 7 © Kevin Fleming/CORBIS; pp. 8 (inset), 12, 15 © Bettmann/CORBIS; p. 8 © CORBIS; pp. 11, 20 © Library of Congress Prints & Photographs Division; p. 16 © Jonathan Blair/CORBIS; p. 19 © Minnesota Historical Society/CORBIS; p. 22 © ChromaZone Images/Index Stock.

Kaplan, Leslie C.
Veterans day / Leslie C. Kaplan.
    p. cm. — (The library of holidays)
Includes bibliographical references and index.
ISBN 0-8239-6660-7 (lib. bdg.)
1. Veterans Day—Juvenile literature. 2. Holidays—Juvenile literature. I. Title. II. Series.
  D671 .K36 2004
  394.264—dc21
                                                          2002008369

Manufactured in the United States of America

Contents

What Is Veterans Day?

On Veterans Day, Americans honor the people who have served in the U.S. military. These people are honored for their service in times of war and peace. This day is also a time to remember the people who have died for America. Veterans Day takes place on November 11. At 11:00 A.M., many people share a moment of silence to remember the fallen soldiers. Throughout the country, parades are held to pay respect to the people who either have fought or are still fighting for the freedom that Americans have today.

This Veterans Day parade took place in St. Louis, Missouri, in 1989. More than 6,000 veterans marched in the parade.

Who Are Veterans?

A veteran might have served in the military either as a soldier or as a doctor or a nurse. Many veterans have died while fighting. Other veterans were wounded but were able to return home. Today there are more than 25 million living American veterans. These veterans have helped to keep peace and have fought in World War I (1914–1918), World War II (1939–1945), the Korean War (1950–1953), the Vietnam War (1965–1973) and the Persian Gulf War (1990–1991).

A veteran is someone who has served in the military in the past or who is serving in the military today. ▶

NEW YORK JOURNAL

EIGHTH EDITION

House by a Vote of 373 to 50 Passes Joint Resolution

WAR IS DECLARED BY U. S.

Interned German Ships Seized by Customs Authorities

Washington, April 6.—After a debate of nearly seventeen hours, the House early to-day passed the resolution previously adopted in the Senate, declaring a state of war against the Government of Germany. The vote was 373 to 50.

The resolution now goes to Vice-President Marshall, who must sign it in formal session of the Senate. It will then be taken before the President for his signature.

Amendments to prevent the use of United States military forces in Europe, Asia or Africa unless directed by Congress were voted down. The resolution adopted by the Senate on Wednesday was approved by the House without the crossing of a "t" or the dotting of an "i."

While the final vote was in progress a tense crowd watched from the galleries. The spectacle was one of the most remarkable, the event certainly the most momentous, in the history of the nation.

The discussion was characterized by many sensations. At one time the presiding officer of the House was compelled to direct the Sergeant at Arms to employ the official mace in enforcing the rules. There was a great deal of tumult, many spirited passages of words

VESSELS IN ALLIES REST PORT HERE TAKEN BEFORE BIG DRIVE

"LOVE U. S. BUT CAN'T VOTE FOR WAR"—MISS RANKIN

The Great War

Although America was at peace in the early 1900s, there was trouble in Europe. Many European leaders wanted land that belonged to other nations. In 1914, war broke out. Germany, Austria, Hungary, and Turkey fought against Great Britain, France, and Russia. More than 30 countries entered the Great War, including the United States. Later this war became known as World War I, or WW I. The war ended in 1918. More than 8 million soldiers had died. These people are remembered on Veterans Day.

◀ *America entered WWI when Germany sank U.S. ships in 1917. The* New York Journal *headline announces the war on Germany.*

Armistice Day

World War I ended officially on November 11, 1918, at 11:00 A.M. Germany signed an **armistice**, or an agreement to stop fighting. In 1919, President Woodrow Wilson made November 11 a holiday. It was called Armistice Day. Each year on that day, Americans remembered the **sacrifices** that soldiers had made during WW I. Officials gave speeches of thanks for the peace that had been won. In 1938, **Congress** voted to make November 11 a national holiday. Armistice Day later became Veterans Day.

On Armistice Day, soldiers who had fought during WW I marched in parades throughout America. ▶

World War II

Veterans Day also honors the soldiers who fought in World War II, or WW II. This war broke out in 1939 when Germany attacked its neighboring countries in Europe, and Japan did the same in Asia. WW II was a much bigger war than WW I, which was fought mainly in Europe. Unfortunately, WW II was fought in Europe, Asia, Africa, and the Pacific Islands. Fifty million people died. Another 28 million were left homeless. One of the worst crimes of WW II was the murder of six million Jews under German leader Adolf Hitler.

◄ *America entered WW II when Japan attacked the U.S. military base in Pearl Harbor, Hawaii, on December 7, 1941.*

A New Name

Congress established Armistice Day to honor WW I veterans. However, there were many veterans who served before WW I and after WW II. Armistice Day failed to honor all those veterans. President Dwight D. Eisenhower recognized this problem. He served as the nation's 34th president from 1953 to 1961. In 1954, he worked with Congress to change the name Armistice Day to Veterans Day. November 11 became a day **dedicated** to honor all American veterans who have served their country during times of war or peace.

President Eisenhower felt strongly about honoring veterans. He said, "to honor veterans...a day dedicated to world peace." ▶

Red Poppies

Since WW I, the red poppy has been a **symbol** for veterans. A bloody battle took place on Flanders Field in Belgium during WW I. The ground in this area held **dormant**, or sleeping, poppy seeds. Soldiers tore up large amounts of ground when they passed through the area. This awakened the poppy seeds. The red flowers bloomed and covered the field. Today people wear paper poppy flowers on Veterans Day to honor and remember the American soldiers who have died for their country.

A green field is covered with red poppies. Veterans groups sell red paper poppies for people to wear on Veterans Day.

Veterans Groups

Some veterans have been wounded so badly in wars that they cannot work. Without **income** from a job, they can't take care of themselves and their families. Veterans groups provide help for these veterans. The American **Legion**, the Veterans of **Foreign** Wars, and the Disabled American Veterans are some of America's veterans groups. Such groups protect the rights of veterans. They arrange medical care for veterans. The groups also set up community programs to increase people's awareness of veterans.

This photo shows disabled WW I veterans making paper poppies. The poppies were sold to raise money for veterans' medical care. ▶

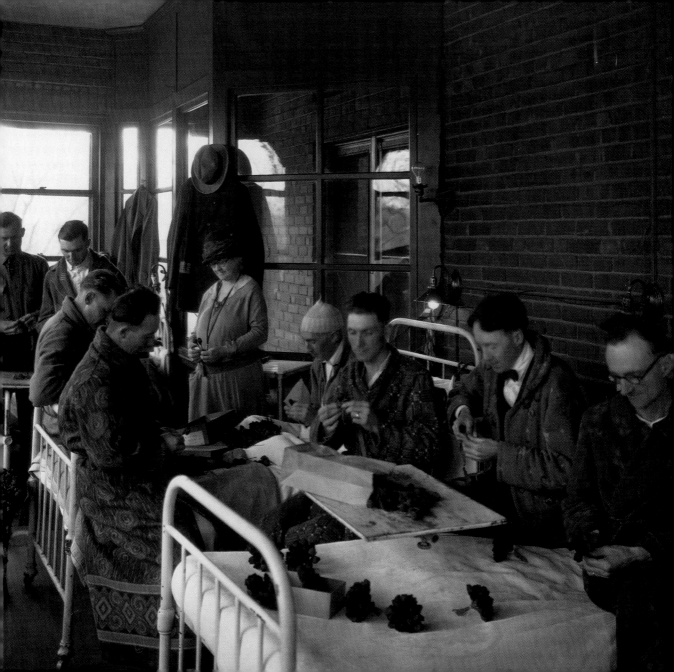

The Tomb of the Unknowns

On Veterans Day, a **ceremony** takes place at the **Tomb** of the Unknown Soldier at the Arlington National Cemetery in Virginia. Three **unidentified** American soldiers are buried there. They represent all the unidentified soldiers who have died fighting for the United States. The first unknown soldier fought in WW I, the second fought in WW II, and the third soldier fought in the Korean War. The U.S. president leads the ceremony at the famous tomb. Flowers are placed on the tomb and a musician plays "Taps" on a bugle.

◄ *President Calvin Coolidge* (center) *led a ceremony at the Tomb of the Unknown Soldier in 1924.*

Celebrating Veterans Day

On November 11, you can celebrate Veterans Day by going to a parade. Listen to a veteran's speech about his **experiences** in the military. Perhaps you might talk to a family member who has fought in a war. Another great way to honor veterans is to fly the American flag. It is a symbol of the veterans' service to America. You can also help disabled veterans by buying a paper poppy to wear on Veterans Day. At 11:00 A.M., join people across America in a moment of silence. It is a time to remember the veterans who have risked their lives to fight for peace.

Glossary

armistice (AR-meh-stehs) An agreement of peace.

ceremony (SER-ih-moh-nee) A special series of acts done on certain occasions.

Congress (KON-gres) The part of the U.S. government that makes laws.

dedicated (DEH-dih-kay-tyd) To devote to a purpose.

dormant (DOR-ment) Resting or inactive.

experiences (ik-SPEER-ee-ents-iz) Knowledge or skills gained by doing or seeing something.

foreign (FOR-in) Outside one's own country.

income (IN-kum) Money received for work.

legion (LEE-jen) A large military force.

sacrifices (SA-krih-fys-iz) Things that have been given up for ideals of belief.

symbol (SIM-bul) An object or a design that stands for something else.

tomb (TOOM) A grave.

unidentified (un-eye-DEN-tih-fyd) Unrecognized or unknown.

Index

Web Sites

Due to the changing nature of Internet links, PowerKids Press has developed an online list of Web sites related to the subject of this book. This site is updated regularly. Please use this link to access the list:

www.powerkidslinks.com/LHOL/veteran/